Philip Johnson
Glass House

Residential Masterpieces 19
Philip Johnson
Glass House

Text by Kengo Kuma
Photographed by Yukio Futagawa
Edited by Yoshio Futagawa
Art direction: Gan Hosoya

Copyright © 2015 A.D.A. EDITA Tokyo Co., Ltd.
3-12-14 Sendagaya, Shibuya-ku, Tokyo 151-0051, Japan
All rights reserved. No part of this publication may be reproduced,
stored in a retrieval system, or transmitted,
in any form or by any means, electronic, mechanical,
photocopying, recording, or otherwise,
without permission in writing from the publisher.

Copyright of photographs
© 2015 GA photographers

Printed and bound in Japan

ISBN 978-4-87140-644-4 C1352

Residential Masterpieces 19

Philip Johnson
Glass House
New Canaan, Connecticut, U.S.A., 1945-96

Text by Kengo Kuma

Photographed by Yukio Futagawa

世界現代住宅全集19
フィリップ・ジョンソン
グラス・ハウス
アメリカ合衆国,コネチカット州,
ニューキャナン　1945-96

文：隈研吾

企画・撮影：二川幸夫
編集：二川由夫

明るくて，悲しい庭──隈 研吾
A Bright, Sad Garden *by Kengo Kuma*

1986年の春，アメリカのバブルのピークに，最初にジョンソンと出会えた。ぼくはコロンビア大学の客員研究員という立場で，ニューヨークでぶらぶらしていた。ロックフェラー財団から，1年分の研究費，生活費をもらえたので，色々な場所を旅して，色々な人に会って，話を聞こうと決めた。建築家というのが，どういう種類の人間かを知りたかったのである。インタヴューを手当たり次第に申し込んだが，ジョンソンだけは，なかなか返事がもらえなかった。当時，ジョンソンは別格であった。20世紀初頭，モダニズム建築をアメリカに持ってきたのが，まずジョンソンであり，80年代，ニューヨークの真ん中に「AT&Tビル」(1984年)を設計したことによって，ポストモダニズムという新しい流行をリードしたのもジョンソンであったし，さらにデコンストラクティビズムという，「ポストモダニズムの次」のムーブメントを，ジョンソンは仕掛けようとしているという話題で，ニューヨークは持ちきりであった。

ジョンソンは，世界のアート界の中心に位置するニューヨークの近代美術館(MoMA)に絶大な影響力を有していた。MoMAに建築セクションをつくったのもジョンソンであった。ミュージアムに建築セクションをつくるということ自体が，ジョンソンの発明であったといっていい。これは「建築のアート化」という，20世紀に特徴的な文化的事件の引き金となった。

建築界最大の怪物であり，黒幕であるから，日本の若造からのインタヴュー依頼に返事が来なくても仕方ないと思った。

しかし，どうしても顔が見たかった。だめもとで，ぼくのパトロンだったロックフェラー財団に頼んでみたら，驚くべきことにすぐに返事が来て，「リップスティックビル」(1986年)の事務所に来いというのである。ミースと一緒に設計した「シーグラムビル」(1958年)から，自分の事務所を，やはり自分の設計した「リップスティックビル」へ引っ越したばかりだったのである。考えてみれば，ロックフェラーは20世紀のアメリカの政治，経済，文化の中心にいて，ジョンソンと二人三脚で歴史をつくったパートナーであり，MoMAを支えてきたのもロックフェラーであるから，このすばやいレスポンスも予想できたことではあった。ロックフェラーがいなかったらMoMAもなかっただろうし，MoMAがなければ，20世紀も別の形をとっていただろう。

「リップスティック」のガラス貼りのミーティングルームに走りこんできた気さくな老人は，テキパキと，そして時にはぐらかし，うっちゃりをいれながら，質問に答えてくれた。「こんなに世界中でたくさん仕事をしているんですね」と驚いたら，「いや，一都市に一つだよ。それ以上頼もうとするとするクライアントはいないよ。みんな飽きっぽいからね。」とシニカルな笑いを浮かべて返してきた。

2度目にあったのは，その次の年，1987年の夏で，ジョンソンの自邸，「グラス・ハウス」(1945-49年)であった。正確にいえば，「グラス・ハウス」という単体の建築に招かれたわけではなく，コネチカット州，ニューキャナンの高級住宅地の，とりわけ中でも緑の濃い森の中の，彼の広大なプロパティに招かれた。数名の建築家とジャーナリストが

It was in the spring of 1986, at the peak of America's economic bubble that I have first met Johnson. I was hanging around in New York as a visiting researcher at Columbia University: with the Rockefeller Foundation paying my research and living expenses for a year, I have decided to travel, meet with people and listen to their stories as much as I could, looking to have an insight into what type of people architects really are. I asked whoever I could contact for an interview, but Johnson was the only one who wouldn't reply. At the time, Johnson was in a class of his own: in the early 20th century, it was Johnson who first brought Modernist architecture to the US; in the 80s it was also Johnson who lead the new trend of Postmodernism when he designed the AT&T Building (1984) in the middle of New York; and again Johnson was the talk of the town as he was said to be launching the next movement 'after the Postmodernism,' the Deconstructivism.

Johnson had an enormous influence on New York's Museum of Modern Art which was the epicenter of the art world. It was him who founded the architecture section in MoMA. The act of creating an architecture section in a museum was itself Johnson's invention, which triggered the cultural phenomenon of the 20th century—'architecture as art.'

Since he was the greatest of the architecture giants and masterminds, it didn't come as a surprise that he wouldn't answer to a request for an interview sent by a Japanese youngster.

But I felt a desperate urge to meet him in person. Having nothing to lose, I took a chance on my patron, the Rockefeller Foundation, to give it a push. To my surprise, the reply came right away, inviting me to his office in the Lipstick Building (1986). He has just moved his own office from the Seagram Building (1958) that he designed with Mies to the Lipstick Building of his own design. When I come to think of it, this quick response wasn't something unexpected since Rockefeller was at the center of politics, economics and culture of 20th century America, as well as being Johnson's partner who worked in tandem to create history, and had been supporting the MoMA. Without Rockefeller there wouldn't have been the MoMA, and without the MoMA the 20th century wouldn't have been the same as it is today.

The unpretentious old man who came running into the glazed meeting room at the Lipstick was quick and forward with his answers, at times dodging or evading my questions. "You've worked on a whole lot of projects around the world," I expressed my amazement. He replied, a cynical smile on his face: "Oh no, just one for each city. No client has ever asked for more than that. They all get bored easily."

The second time I met him was the following year, in the summer of 1987, at his own residence, the Glass House (1945-49). To be precise, I wasn't invited to a single piece of architecture that is the Glass House, but to his vast estate amid the deepest greens of lush foliage in the upscale community of New Canaan, Connecticut. I was there with several architects and journalists.

The Glass House was small. Maybe because my expecta-

一緒だった。
　「グラス・ハウス」は小さかった。期待が大きすぎたということがあるかもしれない。小さくて，わりとダサい家だなあ，と思った。
　広大で隣りが見えないプロパティの中に，いろいろなものが建っていた。池に浮かぶように建てられた，アーチの連続する水上パヴィリオン。彫刻ミュージアム，絵画ミュージアム。どれもミュージアムとかいっているわりには，思ったより小さくて，書き割りのようでもあり，ミニチュアのようでもあった。実際，水上パヴィリオンは通常の建築よりも縮小してつくられて，頭がつかえた。写真ではスケールはわからないものだと気づいた。ジョンソンは，そうやって，20世紀という「写真の時代」を手玉にとったのだ，と実感した。頭をぶつけそうになって，小さなパヴィリオンの中をうろうろするわれわれを見て，ジョンソンは明るく笑っていた。
　「グラス・ハウス」をゆっくり説明してくれるかと思ったが，ちょっと恥ずかしそうに素通りされてしまい，絵画ミュージアムの方に，さっさと歩いていってしまった。
　絵画ミュージアムといっても，建築は小さい。しかし，絵画の量はとてつもなくて，それが，回転式のシステマティックな収蔵システムにしまい込まれているのである。ジョンソンは，その機械を回転させながら，早口で，どんどん絵の説明をはじめた。友人のフランク・ステラの作品をはじめとして，驚くべき量であった。20世紀の絵画史がここに詰まっていると思った。

　しかし，残念ながら，まったく感動がなかった。たくさんありすぎると感じた。たくさんありすぎて，一つひとつがどうでもよく感じられてきた。プロパティの中の建築と同じで，多すぎて，一つひとつがどうでもよく感じられてくるのである。絵画も建築も，すべてがどうでもいいくだらないものに感じられてきた。歴史そのものが，どうしようもない，くだらなくて，安っぽいものに感じられてきた。
　この印象は，18世紀のイギリスの貴族の，風景式庭園と近似している。たくさん貴重なものが集められているのだが，すべてがどうでもよく感じられてくるのである。パヴィリオンに縮小の方法を用いて，錯覚を誘発する点もよく似ている。18世紀の貴族も，そしてジョンソンも，集めれば集めるほど，虚しくなったのだろう。だから，またさらに集めてしまうのである。それによって，増大するのは，コレクションではなく，虚無である。ジョンソン自身が，風景式庭園が好きだともいっている。
　「桂離宮」に似ていないこともない。池を中心とする構成も似ているし，パヴィリオンの小ささも書き割りっぽさもそっくりである。たくさんストーリーもあるし，おもしろいディテールもあるのだが，次第にどうでもよく感じられてくるのである。
　ジョンソンの自邸も，風景式庭園も，「桂離宮」も，どれも社交のための空間ということで総括できる。主人が住むための家ではなく，人をもてなすための家である。主人はそもそも，裕福すぎる自分が恥ずかしいのである。たいした理由もなく，裕福になった自分が恥ずかし

tions were too high. I found the house to be small, and a bit dowdy.

　A variety of structures were built inside the vast property where the neighbors were nowhere in sight: Pavilion in the Pond, a sequence of arches floating on water; the Sculpture Gallery; the Painting Gallery. To me, all of these appeared much smaller than what their names suggested, like miniatures or stage settings. In fact, the Pavilion in the Pond's size was scaled down compared to that of a regular architecture, with its ceiling so low we all bumped our heads. It made me realize that photos do not reflect the real scales of buildings: it was in this way that Johnson has played with the 20th century, an 'age of photography.' Johnson laughed cheerfully as we walked inside the tiny pavilion, hitting our heads on the ceiling.

　Instead of giving us a full interpretive tour of the Glass House as anticipated, he just passed it by with a slight touch of embarrassment, and quickly walked over to the Painting Gallery.

　Despite the fact that it's called the Painting Gallery, the building is small. But the paintings collection is huge, displayed on a system of revolving storage racks. Johnson started to rotate the panels and explain hastily about the paintings one after another. The sheer quantity of paintings, by his friend Frank Stella among others, was utterly impressive: it was literally packed with the history of 20th century paintings.

　However, sadly enough, it left me with no emotion whatsoever. There were just too much. There were too much paintings and none of them seemed to matter anymore. Like those structures in the property there were too much of them that each one of them ceased to matter for me. I began to feel that, paintings and structures alike, everything was pointless and futile. I began to feel that history itself was helpless, worthless and cheap.

　Such impression is reminiscent of the 18th century landscape garden by the British aristocracy, where an array of precious items was assembled but ultimately none of which made any difference at all. How they adopted the method of scaling down sizes to the pavilions to induce a false sense of perspective also bears a strong resemblance. Both the 18th century aristocracy and Johnson probably felt more empty as they amassed their collections, which made them collect even more. In doing so, what gathers more volume is not the collection but a sense of emptiness. In fact, Johnson has once voiced his preference for landscape gardens.

　There's even a certain resemblance to the Katsura Imperial Villa: the layout centered around a pond is similar, and so is the pavilion's small size and stage set-like aspect. Both are rich in stories and interesting details that, with time, make you feel like you couldn't care less.

　Johnson's own residence, the landscape garden, and Katsura Imperial Villa can all be summarized as a space for socializing. Rather than being a house for the owner to live in, it is a house for entertaining guests. The owner is, to start with, embarrassed about himself for being too wealthy. Ashamed of

いのである。だから，たくさん集めて，人に見せる。一つのものにこだわりすぎると，こだわった自分の本性が見透かされてしまうようで，恥ずかしい。だから，ついつい，たくさん集めてしまって，たくさん見せて，自分がどこにいるのかわかりにくくして，ごまかすのである。風景式庭園も，「桂離宮」も，ジョンソンの庭も，同じような韜晦（とうかい）の産物である。

建築家という仕事をしていると，世界の金持ちの家にしばしば招かれる。色々なものを山ほど見せられる。早口で説明される。みんな恥ずかしいから早口になるのである。たくさんあるけれど，実はどれも彼にとってはどうでもいいのである。

ミースが弟子のジョンソンからこの「グラス・ハウス」に招かれて，とても機嫌が悪くなったというのは有名な話である。「天井が高すぎる」といったというが，ぼくはそうは感じなかった。鉄骨の構造体の表現も，ミースの「ファンズワース邸」(1950年)にくらべて切れがなくて，凡庸だった。スティール手りのような中途半端なものが中途半端な高さについているし，床に敷き詰めた赤いレンガもダサい。ミースの緊張感のある「家」と比べようもなかった。庭に付属した，仮設の東屋（パヴィリオン）のようなものだと感じた。ミースもそう感じただろう。

ミースやコルビュジエの時代，すなわち，「サヴォア邸」(1931年)や「バルセロナ・パヴィリオン」(1929年)の時代は，「家」という単体の建築をデザインすることが目的であった。「家」という，自立し，完成度の高い商品を美しくデザインすることが，建築家の最大の目的であった。「商品」特有の，緊張感に富んだ，研ぎ澄まされた構成を，コルもミースも目指していた。

それまでは，建築は「商品」ではなかった。地面とくっついていて，切り離しようがなかった。そもそも売るものではなかった。しかし，コルビュジエやミースは，それを地面から引き剥がして，独立した商品と見立てて，20世紀というすべてが「商品」として売り買いされていく時代の中で，しっかりと商売をしようとたくらんだのである。だから「サヴォア邸」はピロティによって地面と切り離されているし，「バルセロナ・パヴィリオン」は，立派なトラバーチンの基壇によって，大地から切断されているのである。MoMAでジョンソンが仕掛けた「MODERN ARCHITECTURE展」(1932年)の本質は，このような，切断された「商品」を販売するイベントであった。この展覧会が，MoMAのあと，デパートを巡回する予定になっていたというのは，有名な話である。

しかし，「商品」の時代を仕掛けた当のジョンソンには，「商品の時代」が長続きしないことも見えていた。人間はすぐに豊かになりすぎて，「商品」みたいな安っぽいものには見向きもしなくなることがジョンソンには見えていた。

「商品」に飽きたあとに来るのは「土地の時代」である。「不動産」の時代である。18世紀の英国貴族のように，20世紀の人間は土地に執着し始める。田舎に土地を所有していてこそ，貴族と，そして資産家と呼ばれるのである。ジョンソンのニューキャナンの家で，人々を圧

---

oneself for being wealthy for no big reasons. So the owner accumulates a collection and shows it to the guests. An excessive obsession is embarrassing, for it reveals the obsessed one's true nature. Hence the act of over-collecting for massive display with the intent of dissembling one's whereabouts. The landscape garden, Katsura Imperial Villa and Johnson's garden are all products of similar self-concealment.

Being a practicing architect, I am often invited to the homes of the world's wealthiest. Who would show me loads of different things. And would explain them in a hasty manner. They're all in a haste because they feel embarrassed. They have plenty, but in fact none of them matters to them.

There's this well-known story about Mies being invited by his disciple Johnson to the Glass House and getting in an awfully bad mood. He's said to have said "the ceiling is too high," but that wasn't what I thought. The expression of its steel-frame structure was, compared to that of Mies' Farnsworth House (1950), mediocre and less sharp. Something like an odd-looking steel railing is mounted at an odd height; the red bricks covering the floor look dowdy. It was nothing compared to the intensity in Mies' 'house.' For me it appeared as a sort of a temporary pavilion that furnishes the garden. And Mies would have felt the same way.

In Mies' and Le Corbusier's time, back in the days of Villa Savoye (1931) and Barcelona Pavilion (1929), it was all about designing a 'house' as a single piece of architecture. An architect's ultimate goal was to design a beautiful, independent and perfectly executed merchandise that is a 'house.' Both Le Corbusier and Mies were in pursuit of a highly intense, refined composition characteristic of the 'merchandise.'

Before them, architecture was not a 'merchandise.' It was something that stayed fixed to the ground and there was no way they could be separated. And it wasn't something that could be sold in the first place. But Le Corbusier and Mies pulled it off from the ground and presented it as an independent product in their strategy of running a steady business in an era that is the 20th century when everything was bought and sold as 'merchandise.' That's why Villa Savoye is separated from the ground by the piloti and why Barcelona Pavilion is severed from the earth by the spectacular plinth of travertine. The MODERN ARCHITECTURE exhibition (1932) curated by Johnson at MoMA was essentially an event promoting the sales of such severed 'merchandise.' It's a well-known fact that this exhibition was originally supposed to be touring department stores after MoMA.

But in the eyes of Johnson who was the very author of the era of 'merchandise' it was obvious that the 'era of merchandise' wouldn't last for long. Johnson foresaw that people would quickly become exceedingly rich and soon start to disdain cheap things like 'merchandise.'

After people grew tired of 'merchandise' came the 'era of the land.' An era of the 'real estate.' Like the 18th century British aristocracy, people of the 20th century began to grow attached to the land. A person is deemed an aristocrat or a

倒するのは，建築ではなく土地である。建築は土地に従属し，土地の美しさを飾り立てるために建てられた。ミース流の基壇は消失し，「グラス・ハウス」は土地と一つになる。土地に付加価値を与えるための，ガーデンパーティのための仮設の東屋のようなゆるい風情を呈する。そこには「バルセロナ・パヴィリオン」の荘厳な基壇もなく，「ファンズワース邸」の浮いた床もなく，赤レンガ敷の床は地面と一体化して，手すりが地面と建築とをつなぎとめ，すべてがユルユルで，悪くいえば緊張感に欠けてダサくて，よくいえば，あったかくて，癒される。

その東屋つきの土地の上で行われるのが，社交である。商品の時代のあとに，土地の時代が来て，そのあとに社交の時代が来ることが，ジョンソンには見えていた。社交の小道具となるのは，商品ではなく，アートである。アートは社交に従属している。だから，たくさん集められるけれども，どんどん小さく感じられて，人々を動かすことがない。

社交の底に流れているのは，一種のニヒリズムである。絶望である。商品にも絶望し，土地にも絶望し，その絶望という大前提の上で，人を招きもてなすのである。ここにアメリカという事情もある。アメリカでは工業化社会，すなわち商品の時代のあとに，商品の没落がきて，その後に土地の時代，そして社交の時代がやってきた。商品への欲望を共有することで，人をつなぎとめる時代のあとに，土地と社交で人々はつながろうとした。アメリカ以外の多くの場所では，土地とコミュニティとは分かちがたく結合していて，社交の場を人為的につくらなくても，人々がつながる途は色々とあった。商品の時代の中でも，絆は消滅せずに残っていたのである。

しかし，アメリカでは土地が広すぎて，その土地には人々をつなぐだけの粘性がなかった。それゆえに，人為的に，そこに絆を創出する装置を埋め込む必要があったのである。ゲーテッドコミュニティも，パーティのための庭も，そのような装置として，アメリカの大地が必要としていたものだった。ジョンソンにはアメリカという土地が，どれだけパサついていて，粘り気がないかがよくわかっていたのである。

ジョンソンは実際に，この庭でクライアントをもてなし，多くの建築の学生を，この土地に招いた。華やかな美女も呼ばれ，大量の酒が供された。自分は美女にはあまり興味がなかったが，庭を飾るために，美女も必要だと考えた。そのもてなしのお皿の一つが，建築であった。

建築がそこまで墜ちたともいえる。アートも墜ちた。豊かさのはてにそのような社交の時間が残った。その時間は決して暗いものではなく，奇妙な明るさに包まれている。「グラス・ハウス」は，とても明るくて，ゆるくて，悲しい家であった。

man of wealth only when he owns a plot of land in the countryside. What overwhelms the visitors at Johnson's house in New Canaan is the land rather than the architecture. Architecture is subordinated to the land, built for the purpose of decorating the beauty of the land. The Mies-esque plinth is lost, and the Glass House becomes one with the land. It puts on a loose, indolent atmosphere, like a temporary pavilion for garden parties that is built to add value to the land. No hints of the awe-inspiring plinth of Barcelona Pavilion or the floating floor of Farnsworth House are to be found: the red brick-covered floor integrates with the land; the handrail anchors the architecture to the ground; everything is loose and slack—putting it worse, lame and lacking intensity, and putting it better, warm and healing.

Then, performed on such land adorned with a pavilion, is socializing. After the era of merchandise comes the era of the land, followed by the era of socializing, and Johnson knew it all. The gadget used in socializing is art, not merchandise. Art is subordinated to socializing. So, although it can be gathered in great quantities, its presence diminishes contrastingly, unable to move people.

What lies in the depth of socializing is a certain type of nihilism. And despair. Out of despair over merchandise, over the land, and on the basic premise of such despair, the owner invites people and entertains them. Coupled with that is a situation unique to the US—in America, the industrialized society, that is, the era of merchandise, was followed by the fall of the merchandise, then came the era of the land, and the era of socializing. After an era when people linked themselves by sharing their desire for merchandise, they then tried to connect with each other through the land and through socializing. In many places outside the US, land was intricately linked with community, and there were a variety of ways people could stay connected without having to artificially create a place for socializing. Human bond was well and alive in an era of merchandise.

However in America the land was so vast that it simply didn't have enough viscosity to keep their people connected. Hence the need to embed a device that would artificially create a bond there. Gated communities and gardens for parties were such devices that the American land needed. Johnson was well aware of how land in America was dry and lacked viscosity.

In real life Johnson entertained his clients in this garden and invited many architecture students to this estate. Beautiful girls were called upon and alcohol flowed generously. Though not interested in beautiful girls personally, he nevertheless believed that beauties were necessary to decorate the garden. And architecture was just one dish served in such banquet.

One could argue that architecture has fallen that deep. Art has fallen just the same. At the end of affluence all that remained was such hours of socializing. These hours aren't dark in any way, and are wrapped in strange, bright light. The Glass House was a very bright, loose and sad house.

English translation by Lisa Tani

Landscape on northwest

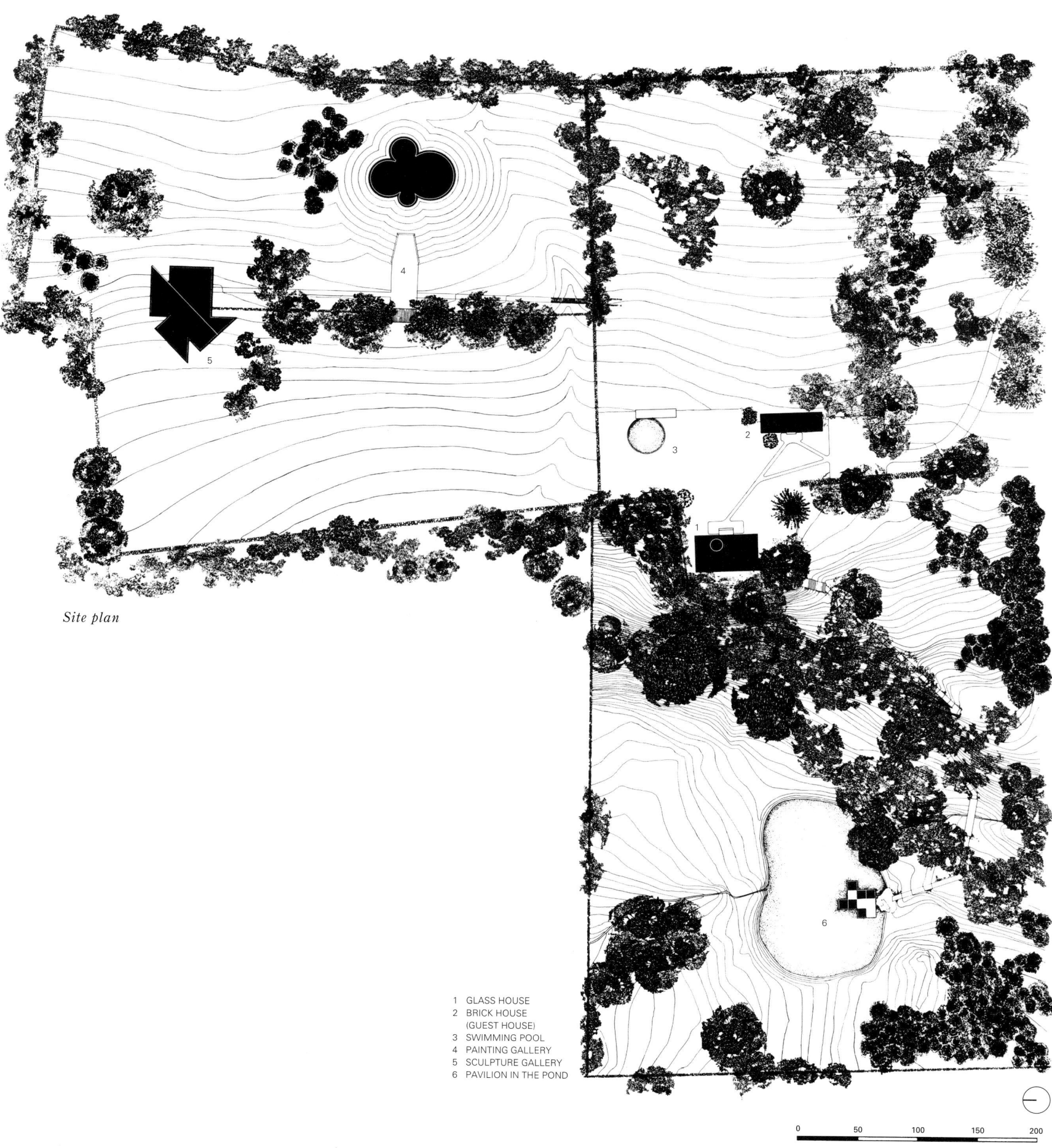

Site plan

1 GLASS HOUSE
2 BRICK HOUSE (GUEST HOUSE)
3 SWIMMING POOL
4 PAINTING GALLERY
5 SCULPTURE GALLERY
6 PAVILION IN THE POND

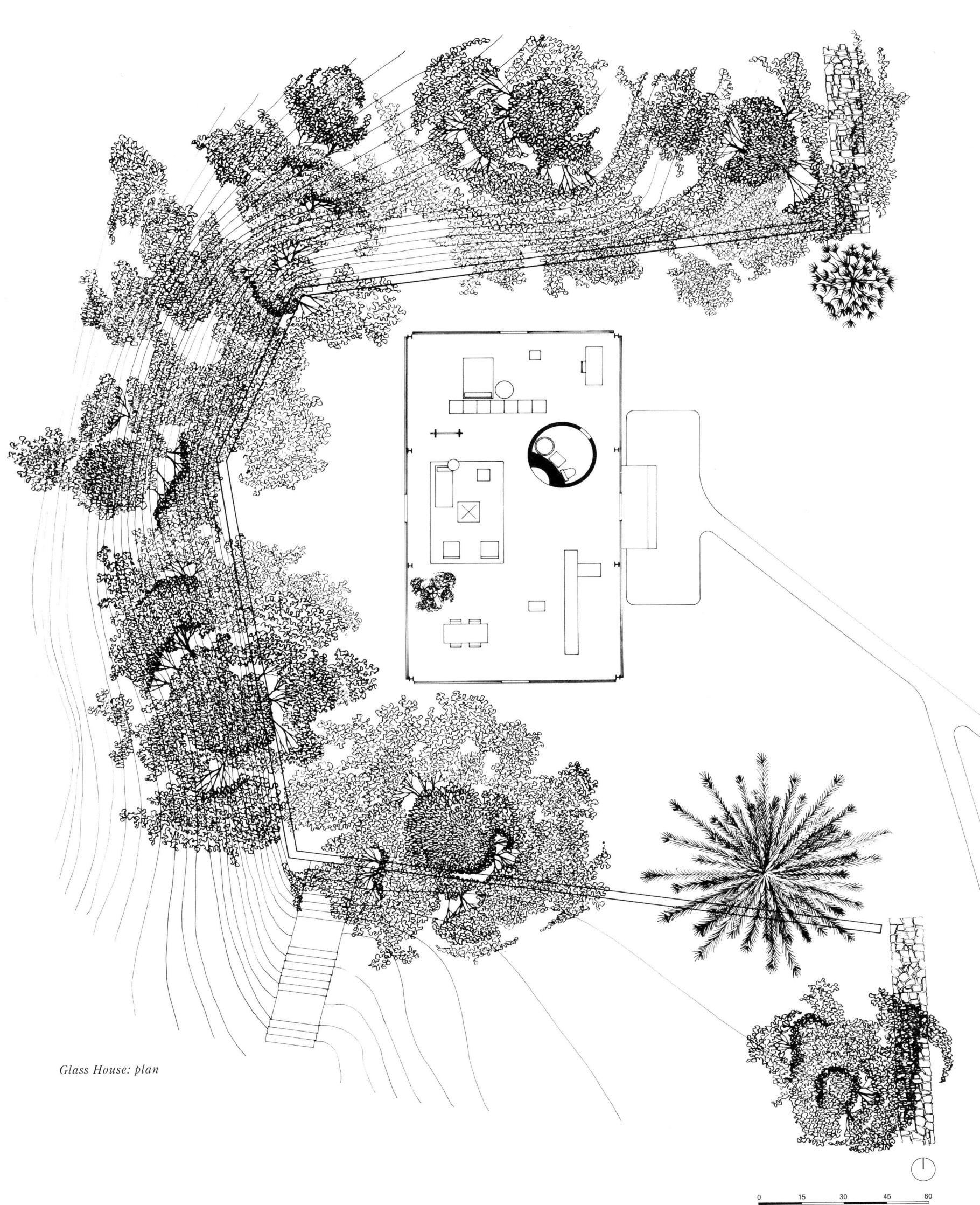

Glass House: plan

Approach to Glass House (1945-49). Circular sculpture of concrete 'Untitled' by Donald Judd on right

Garden. Glass House (left) and Sculpture Gallery (far right)

Garden with Brick House (1949, left), swimming pool (1955) and Glass House (right)

Path from Brick House to Glass House

Glass House in summer

Glass House in spring

Glass House: living room. Furniture designed by Mies van der Rohe

Glass House: view from dining room toward living room. Fireplace on right

Glass House: living room. Behind fireplace, circular brick wall houses bathroom

Glazed perimeter wall

Glass House: bedroom (right) and living room (left)

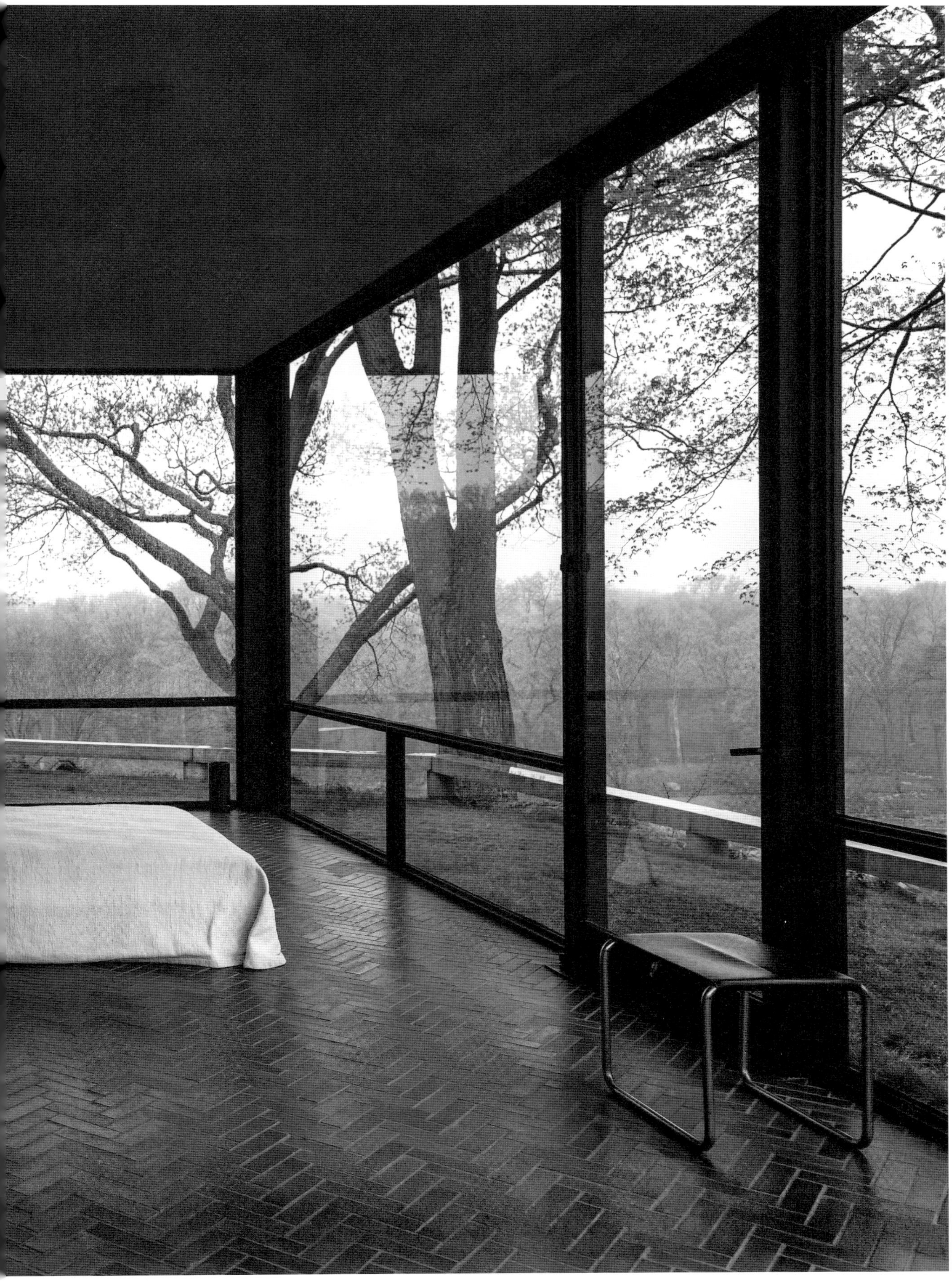

Glass House: bedroom. View toward study

Study

Glass House: living room. Kitchen on left

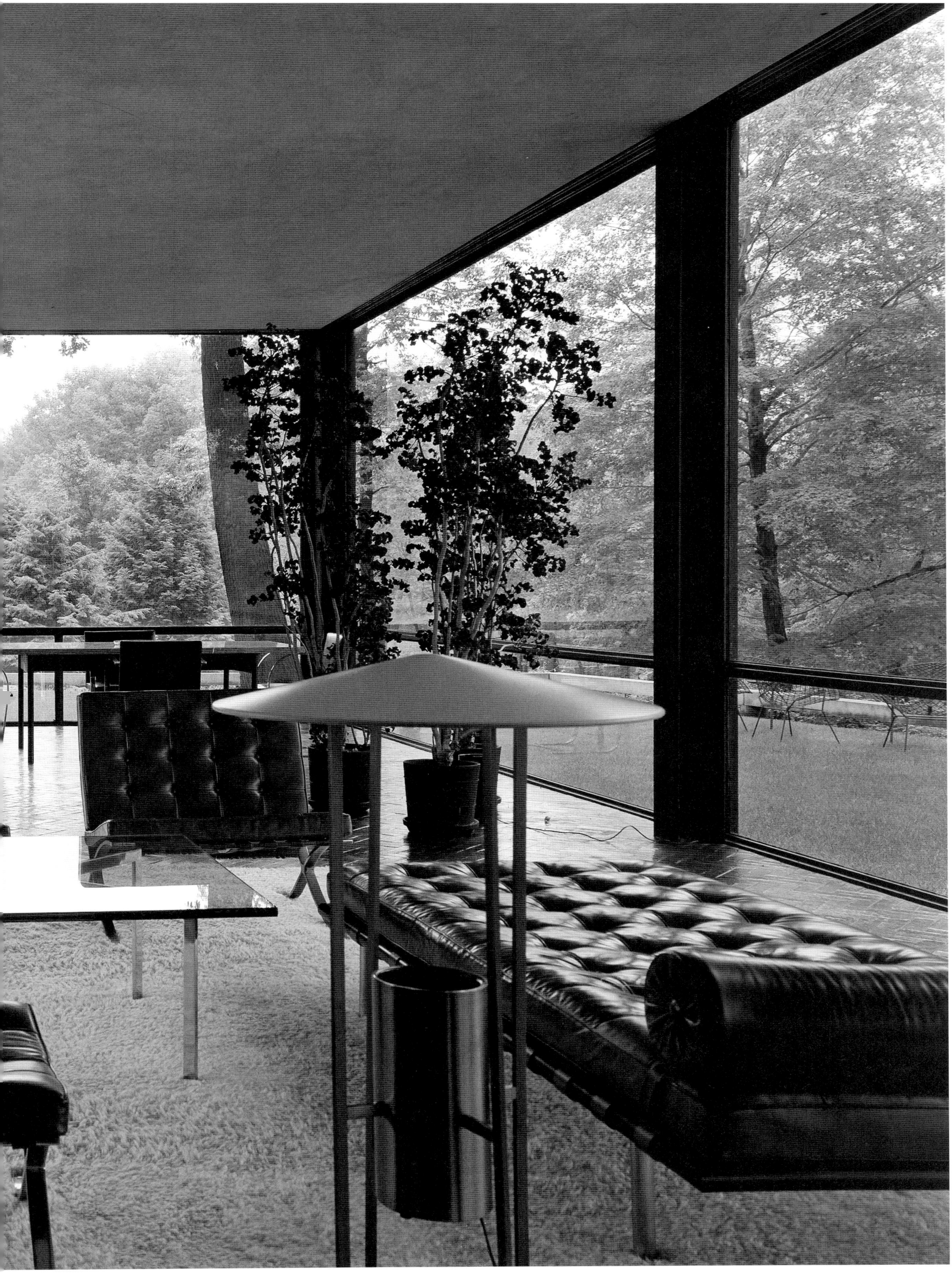

Glass House: kitchen

'Two Circus Women' by Elie Nadelman

Glass House: view from west

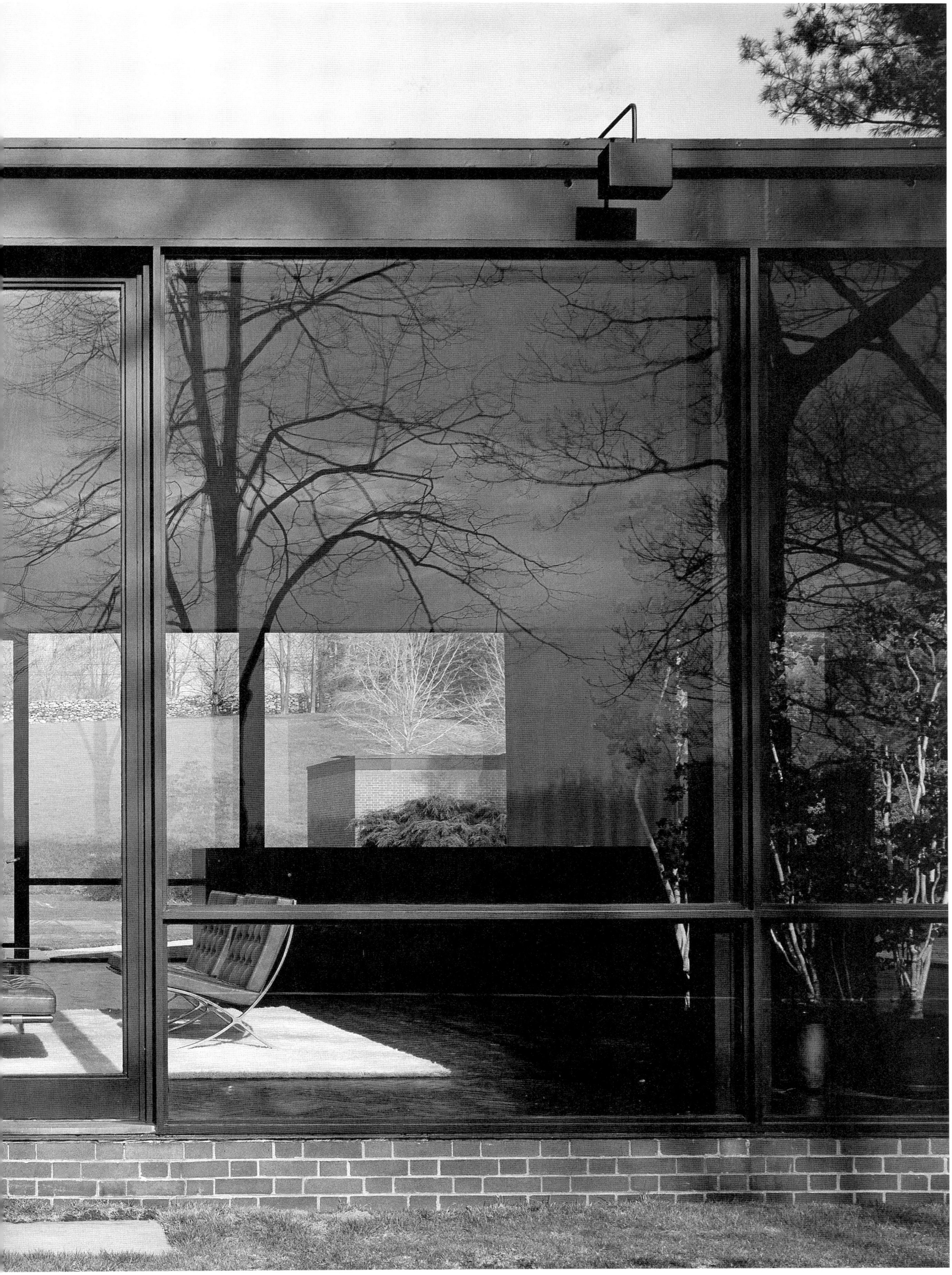

Glass House: west lawn in fall

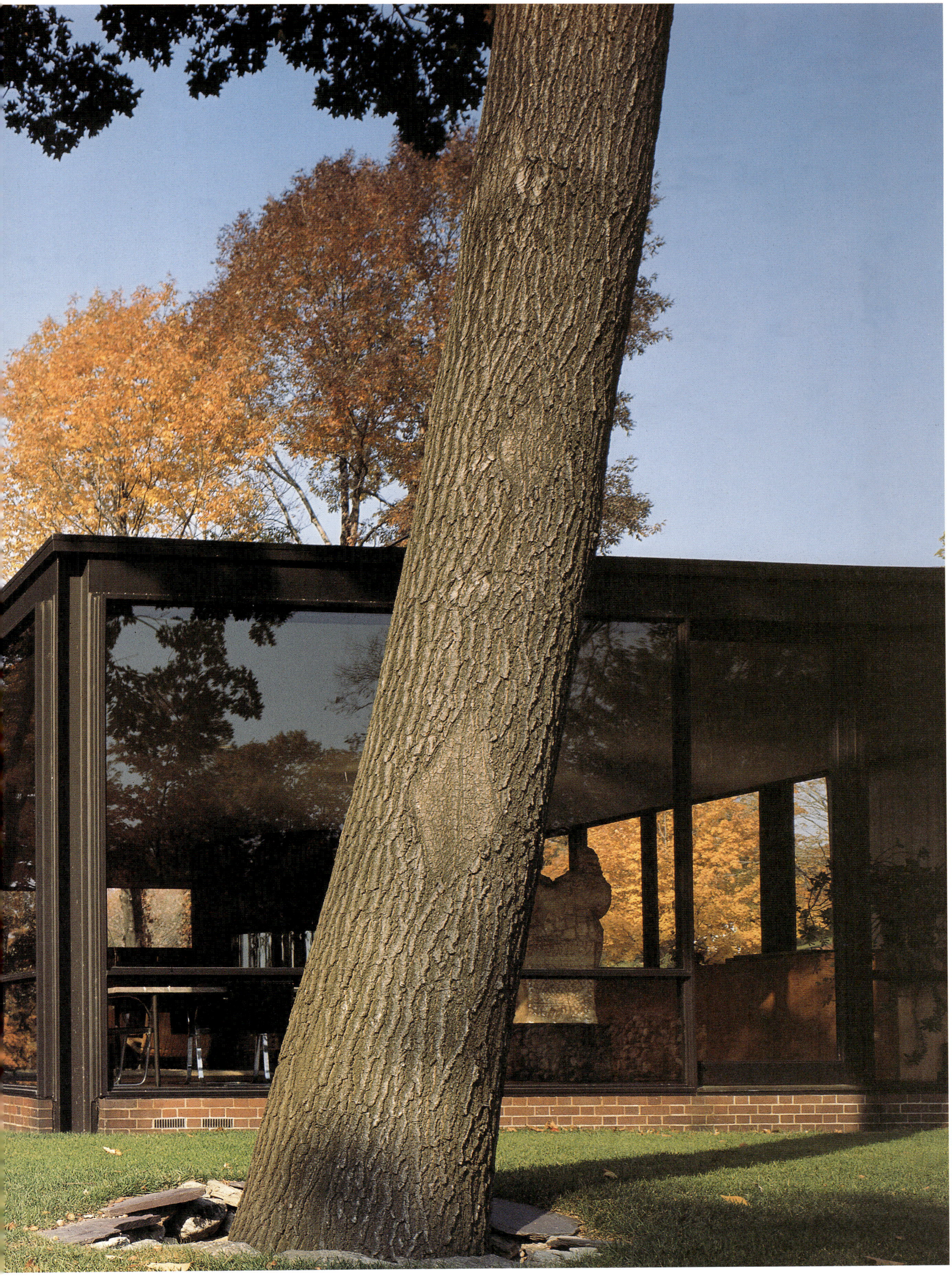

Glass House (left) and Brick House (right)

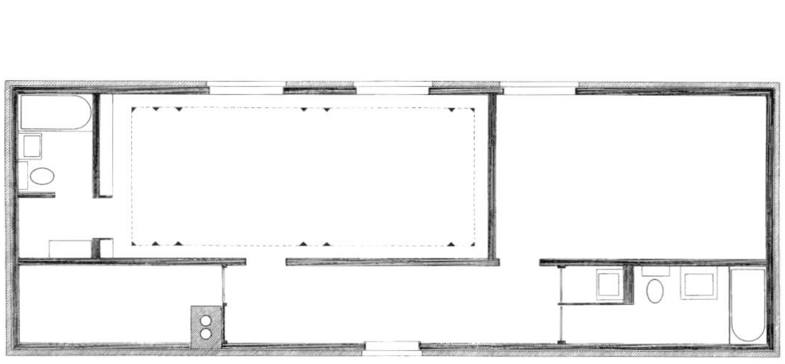

Brick House (guest house): plan and section

Brick House (guest house): bedroom

Brick House (left) and Glass House (right)

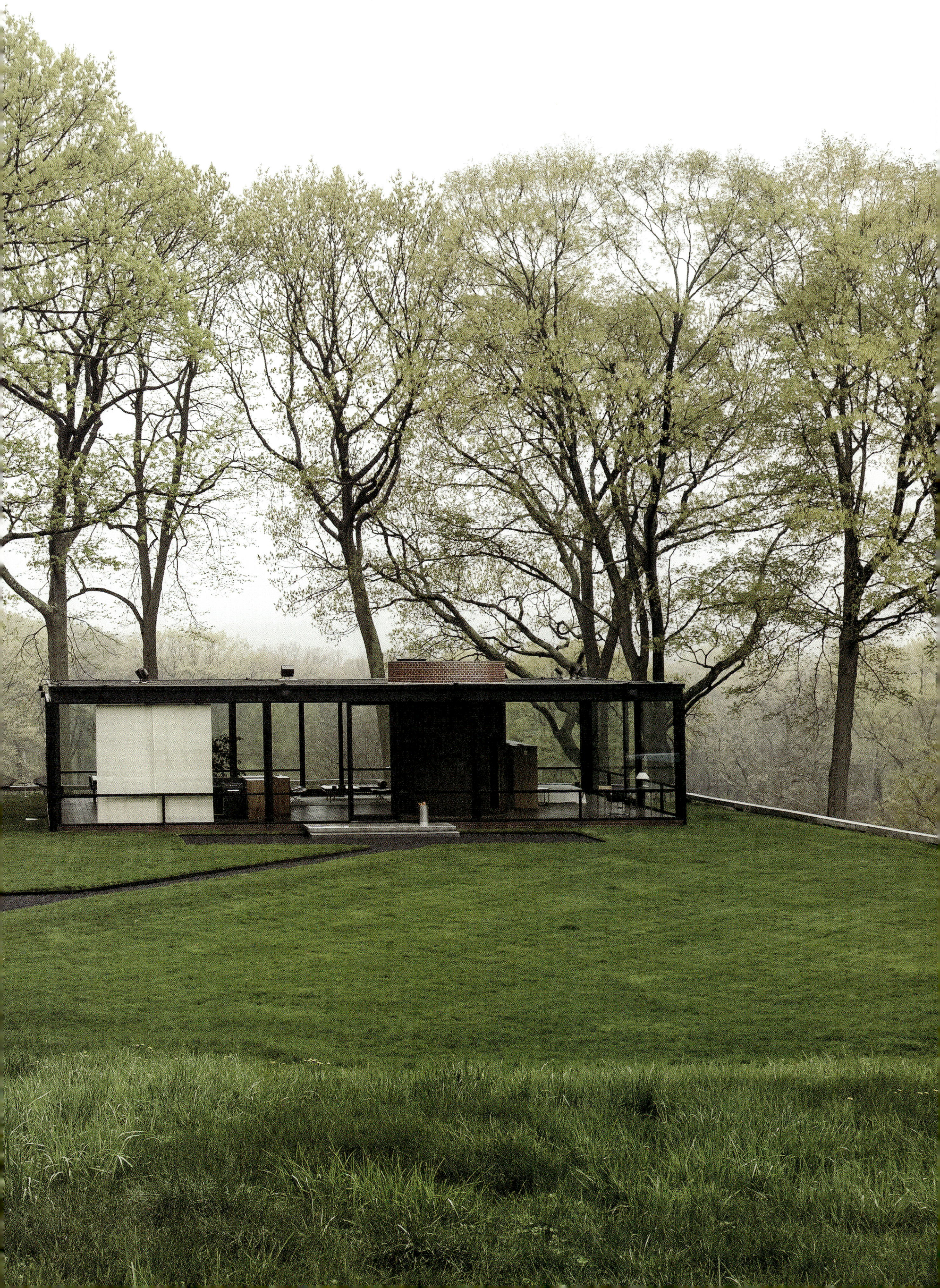

Corner of Glass House (right) and Sculpture Gallery (1970, left)

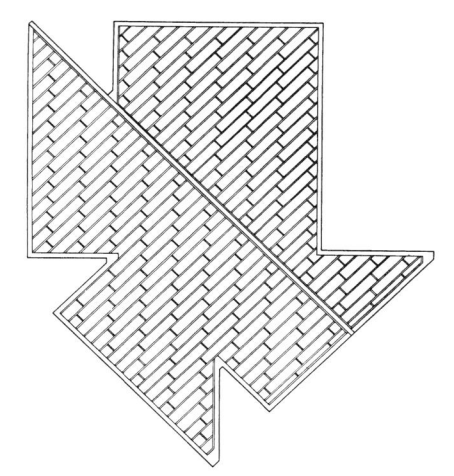

Sculpture Gallery: ceiling

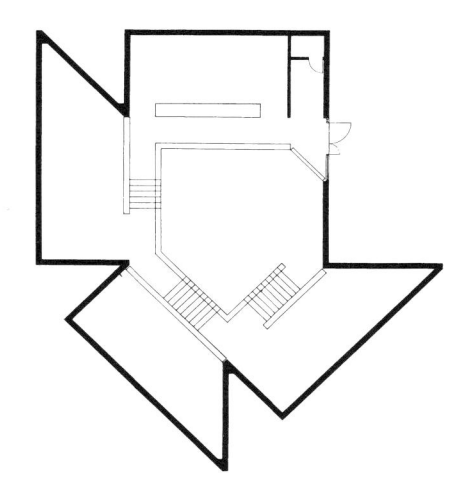

First floor

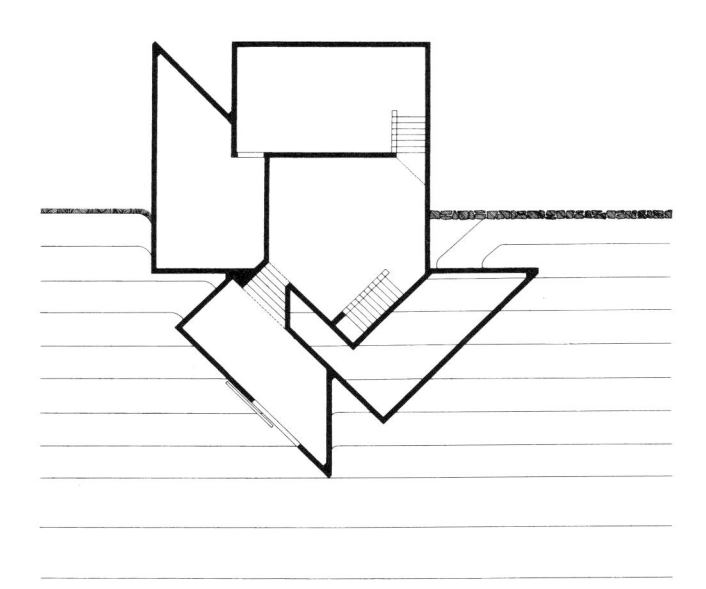

Basement

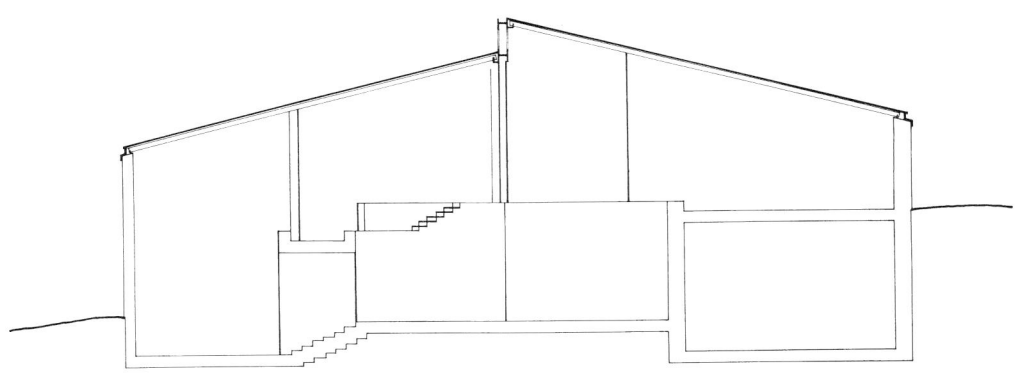

Sculpture Gallery: section

Approach to Sculpture Gallery. Painting Gallery (1965) on right

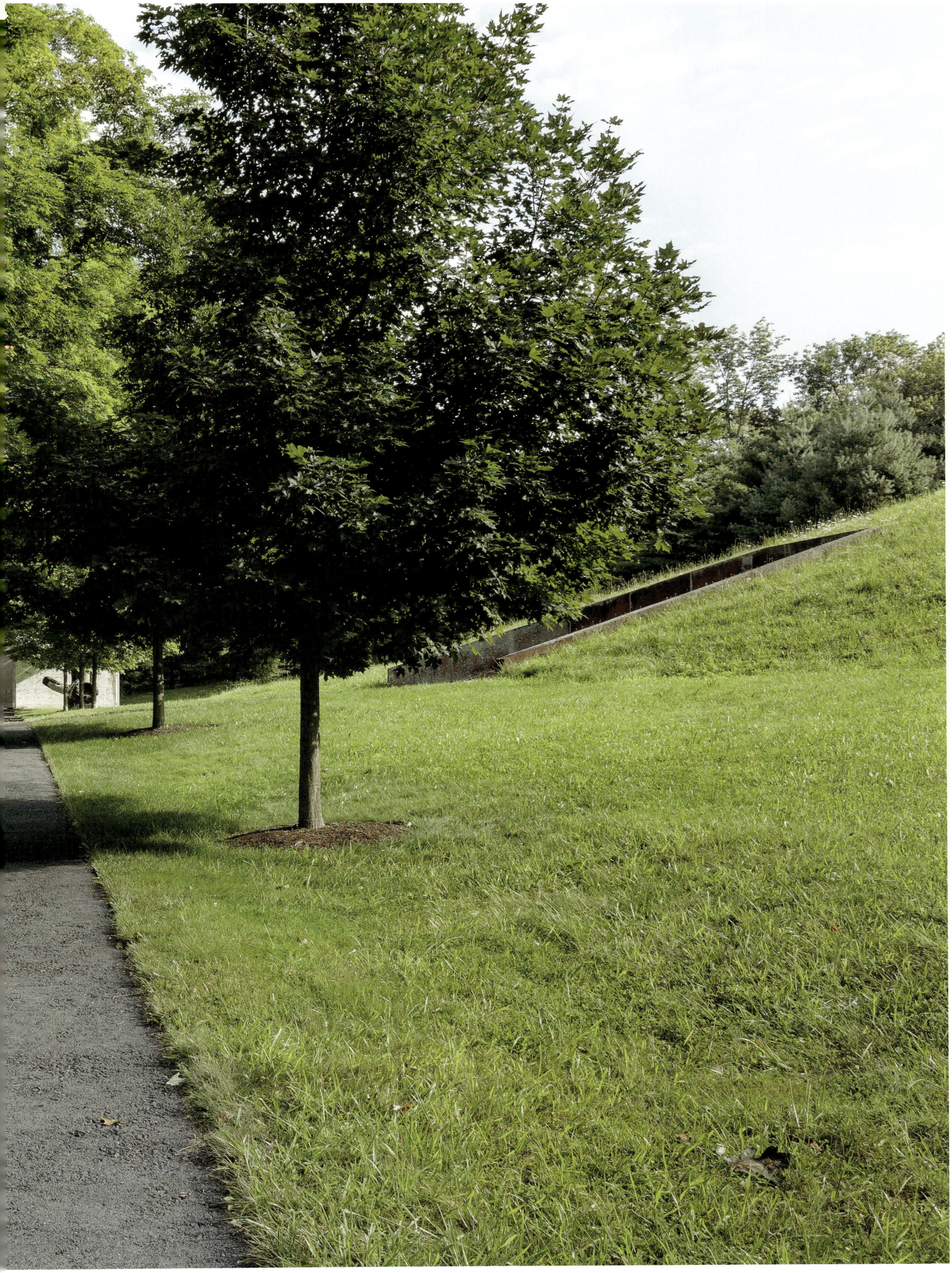

Sculpture Gallery: entrance on center

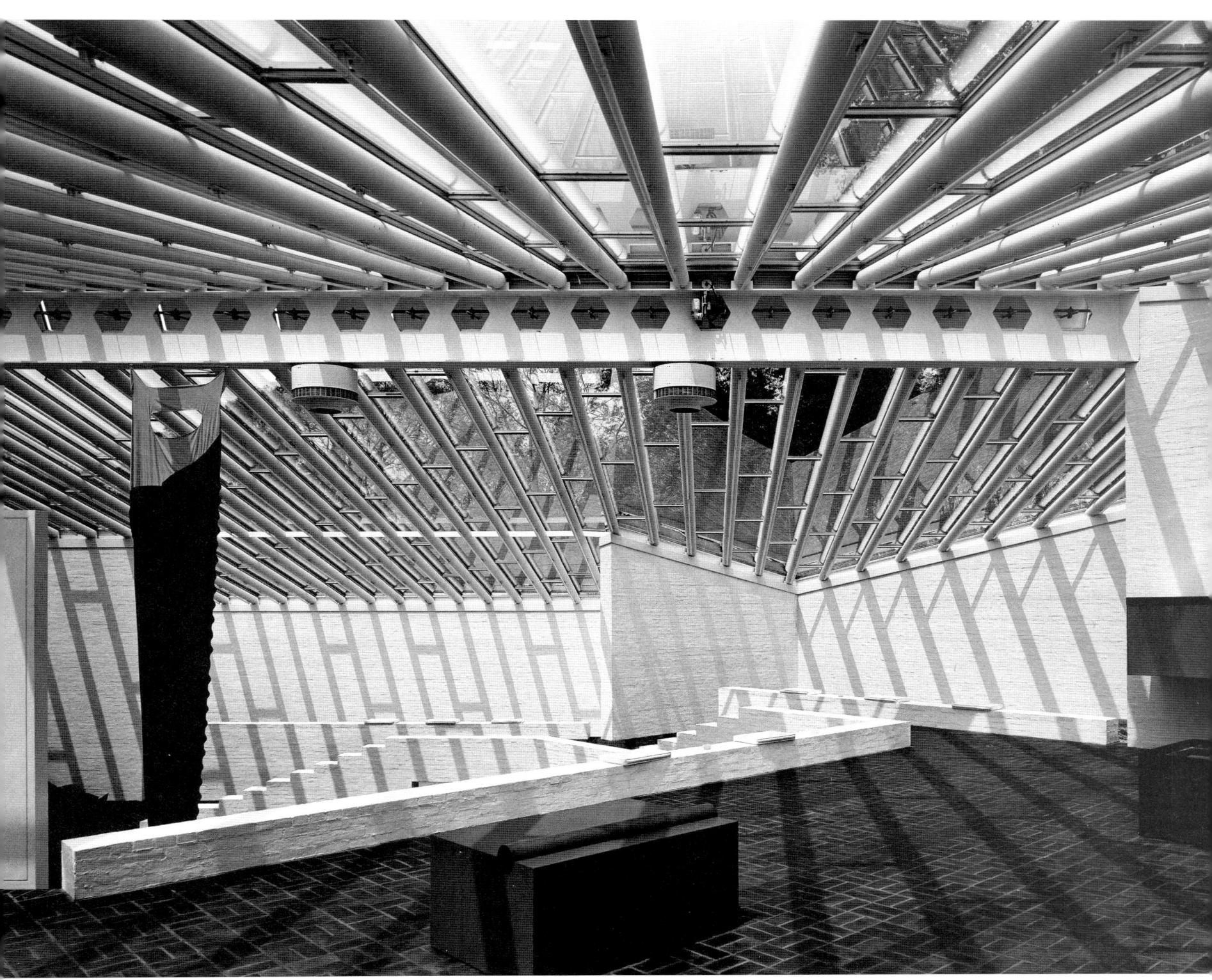

Entrance level

Sculpture Gallery: view from entrance

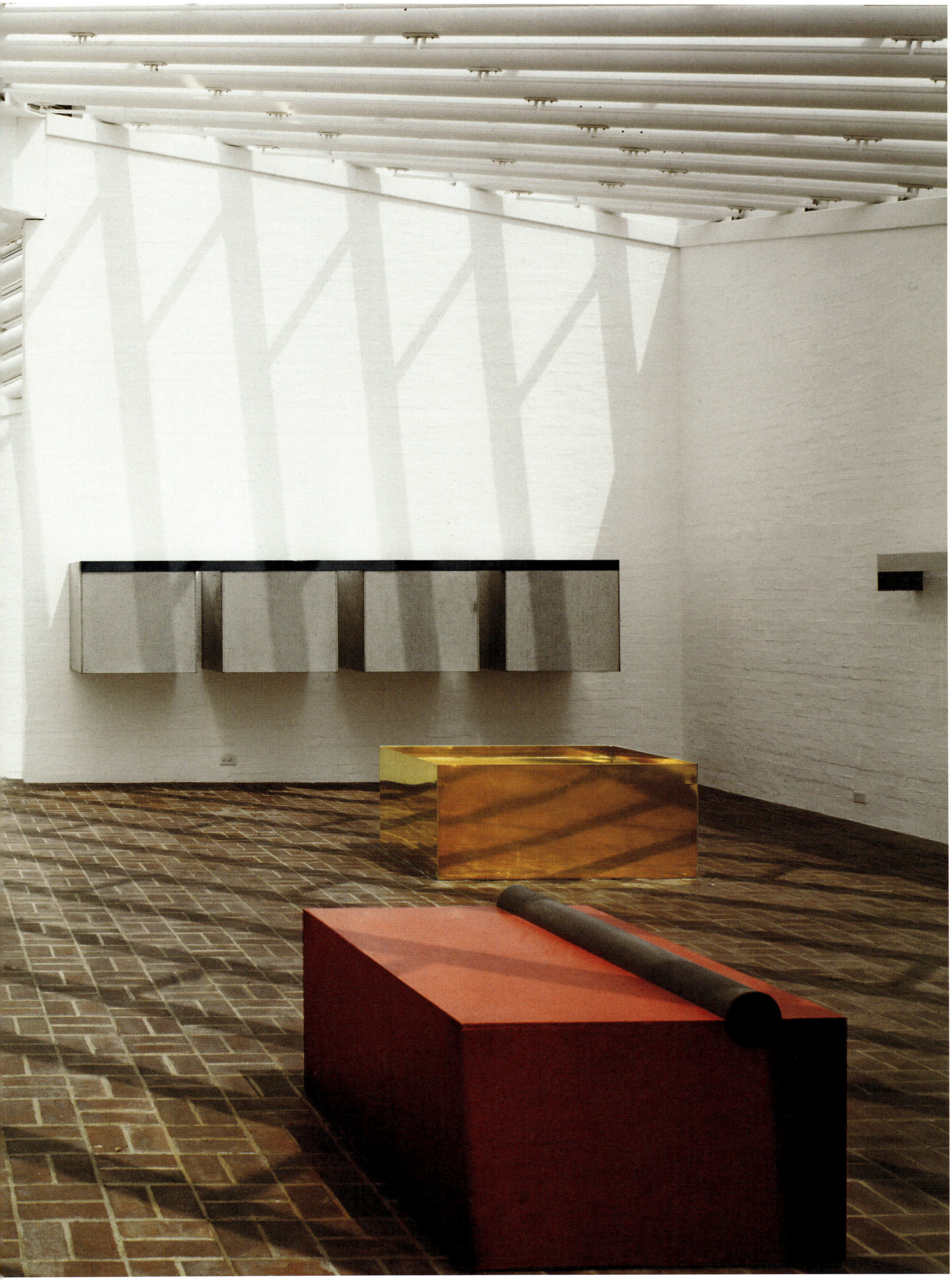

Sculpture Gallery: staircase to lower level

Staircase: entrance on right

Sculpture Gallery: sculptures are installed under natural light from glazed roof

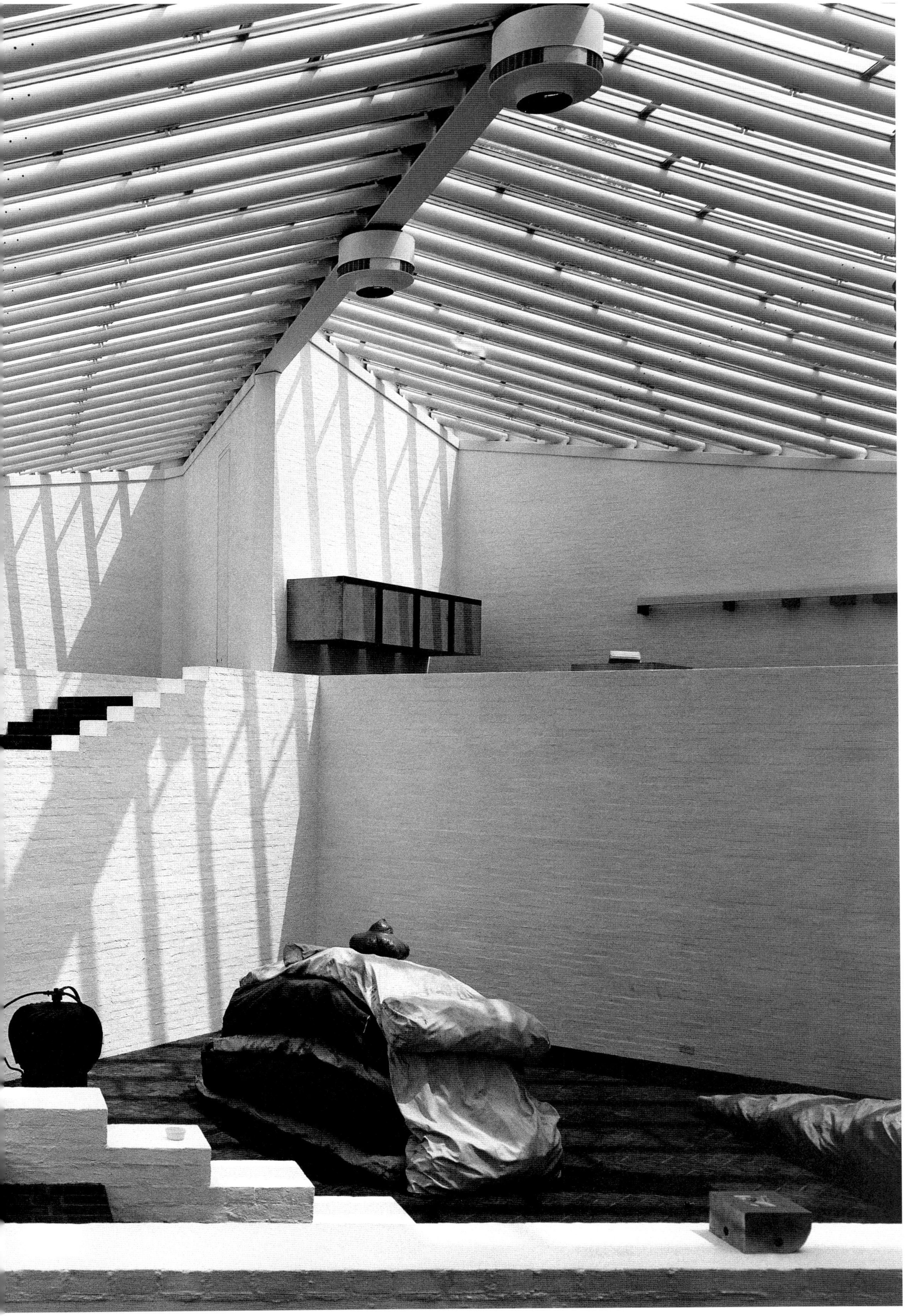

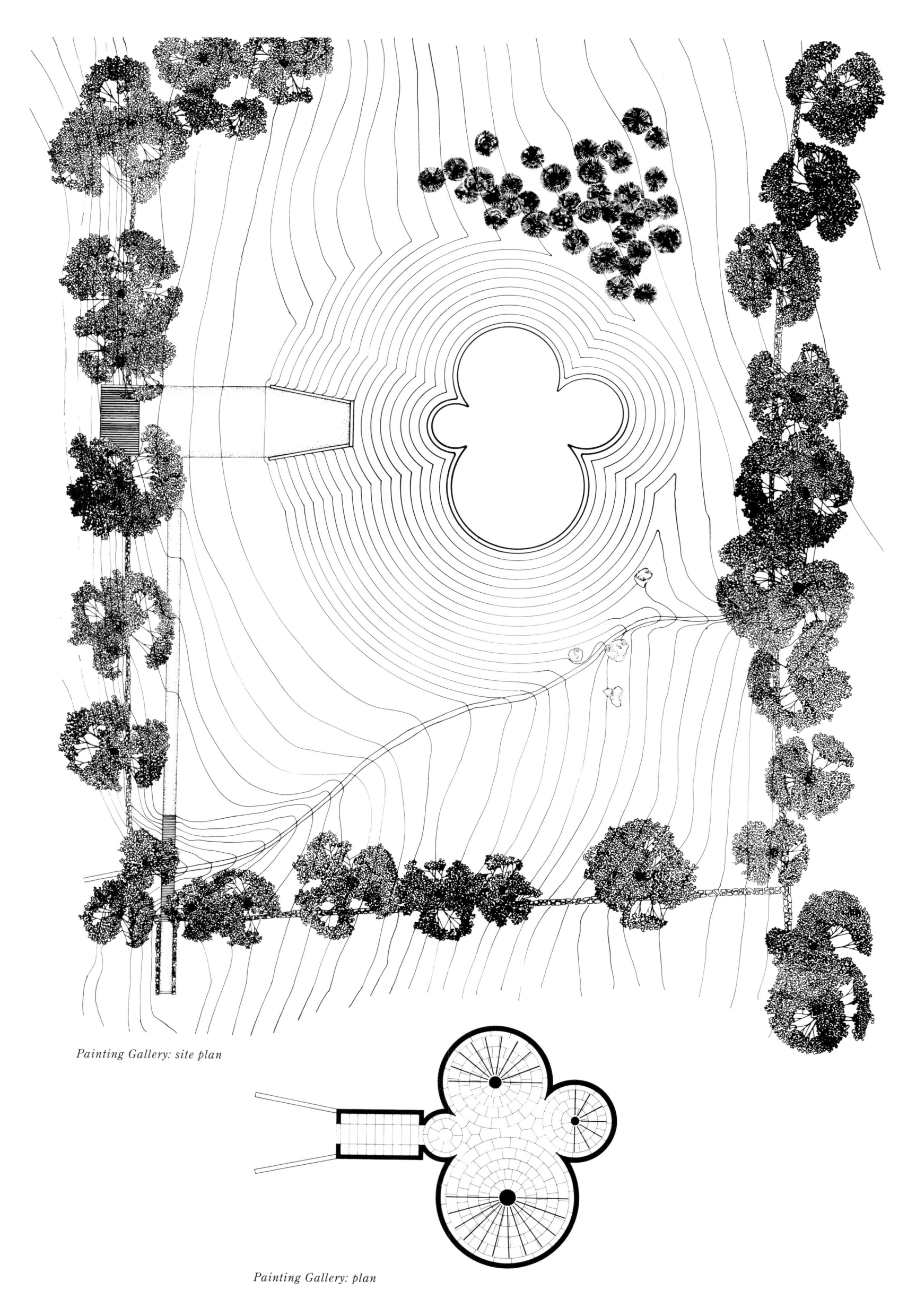

Painting Gallery: site plan

Painting Gallery: plan

Painting Gallery: entrance

Painting Gallery: entrance hall

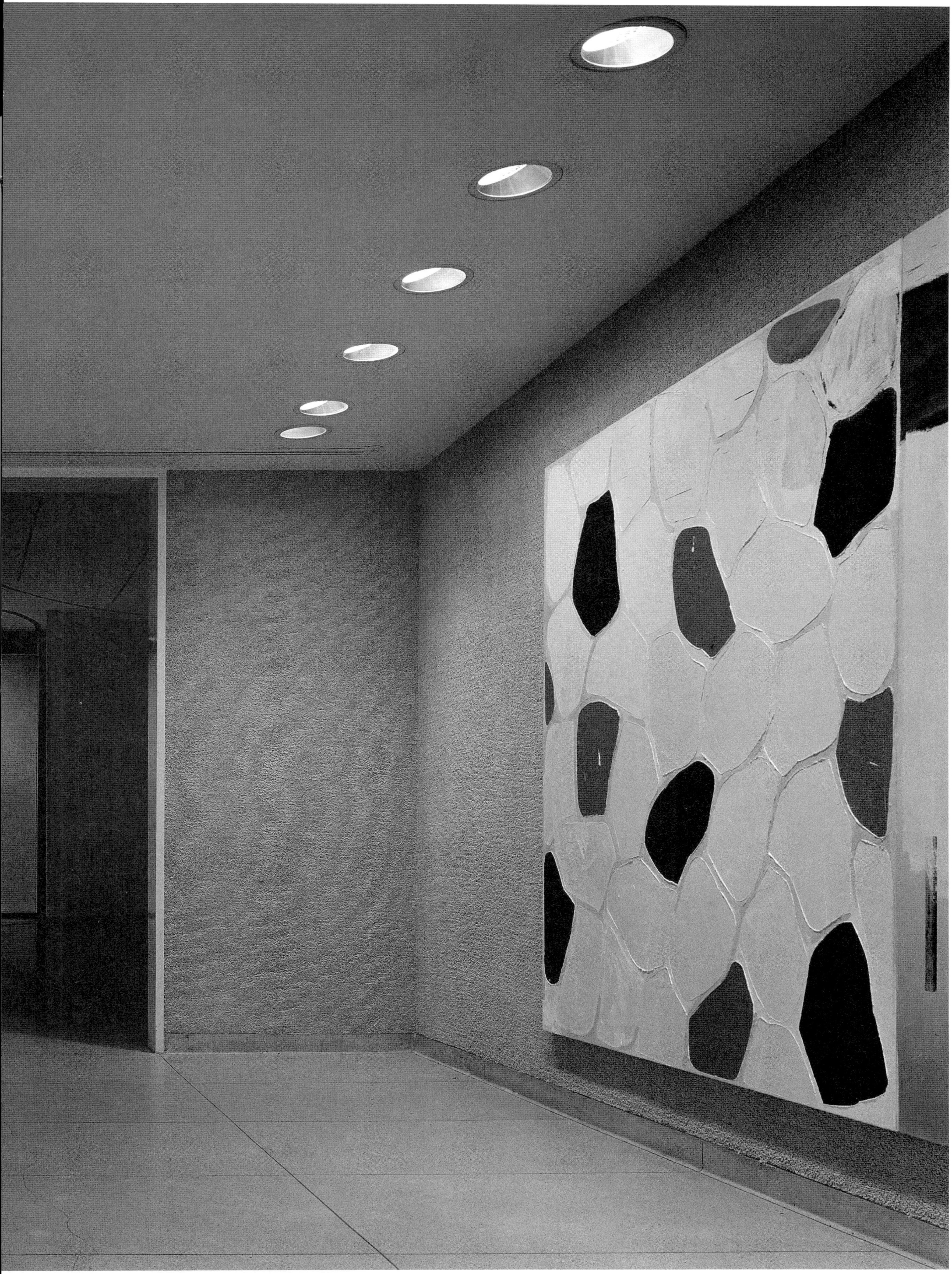

Painting Gallery

65

View toward Studio (1980) from Glass House

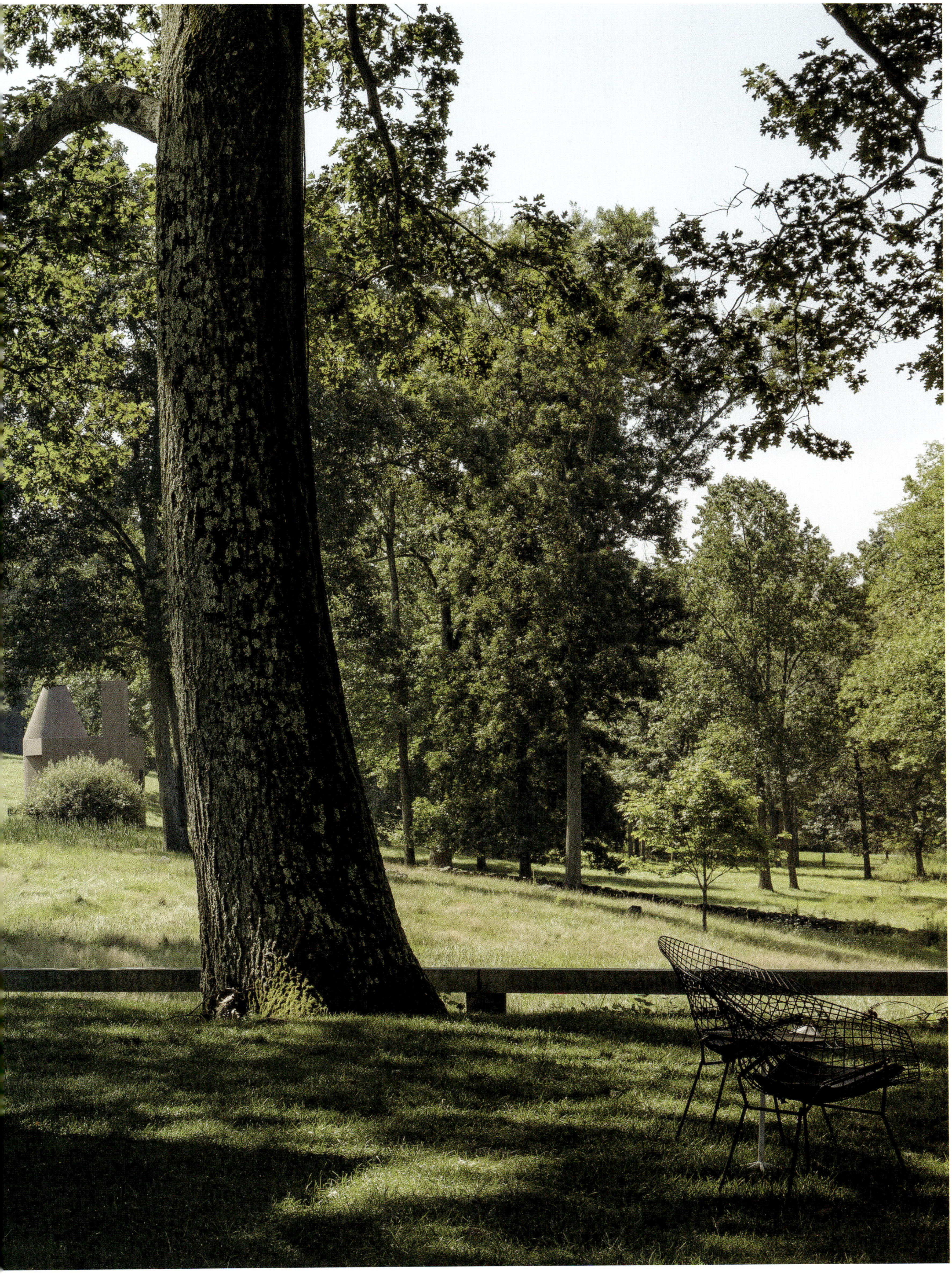

Studio (left) and Ghost House (1984, right)

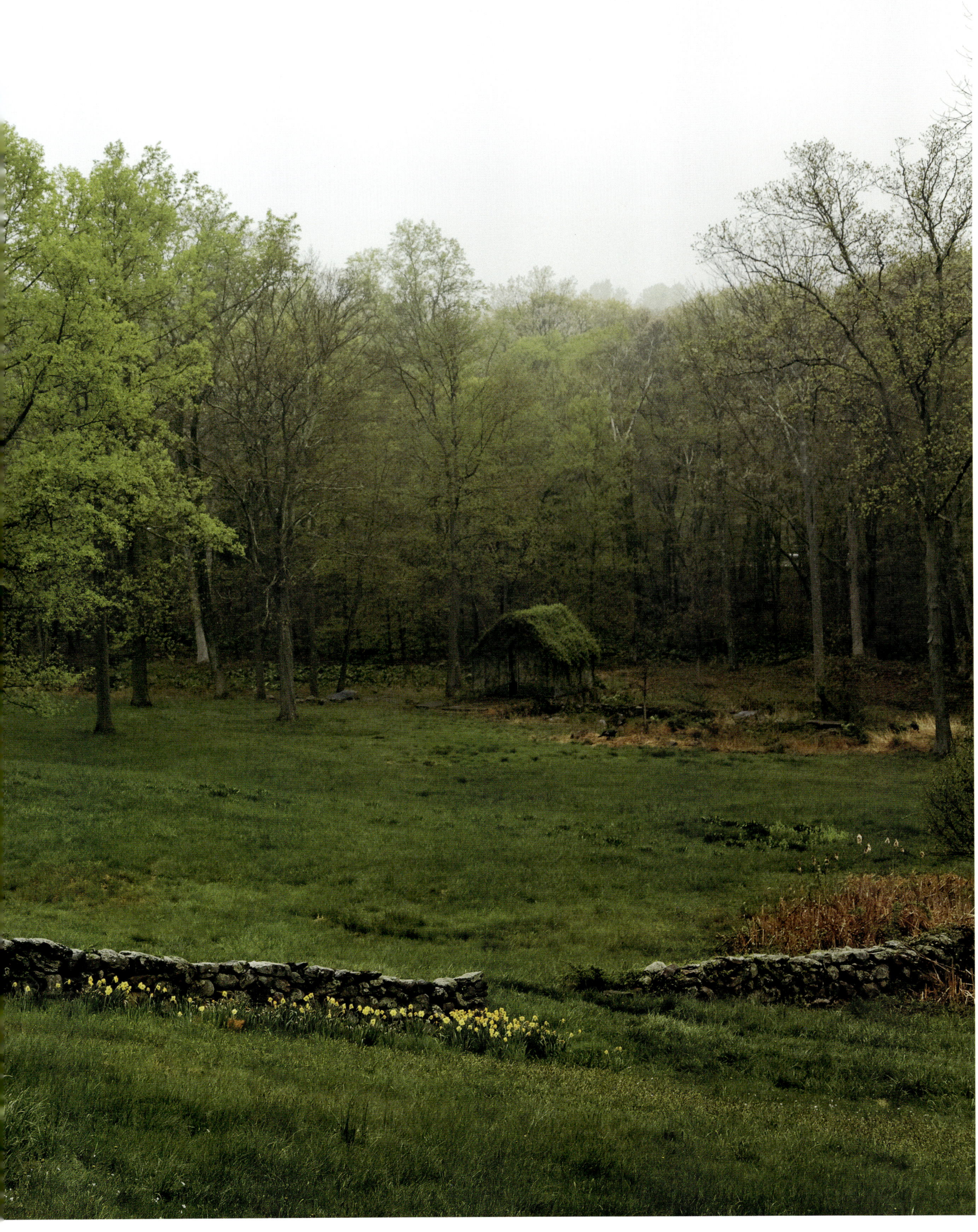

Studio

Da Monsta (1995)

Pavilion in the Pond

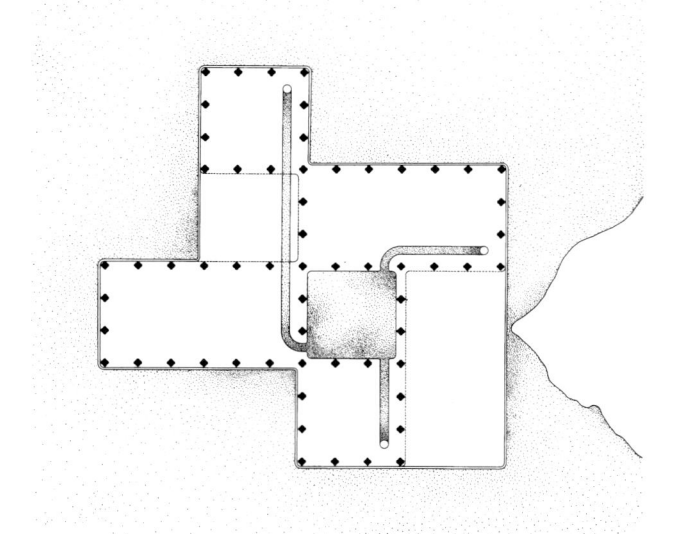

Pavilion in the Pond (1962). View toward Glass House on left above

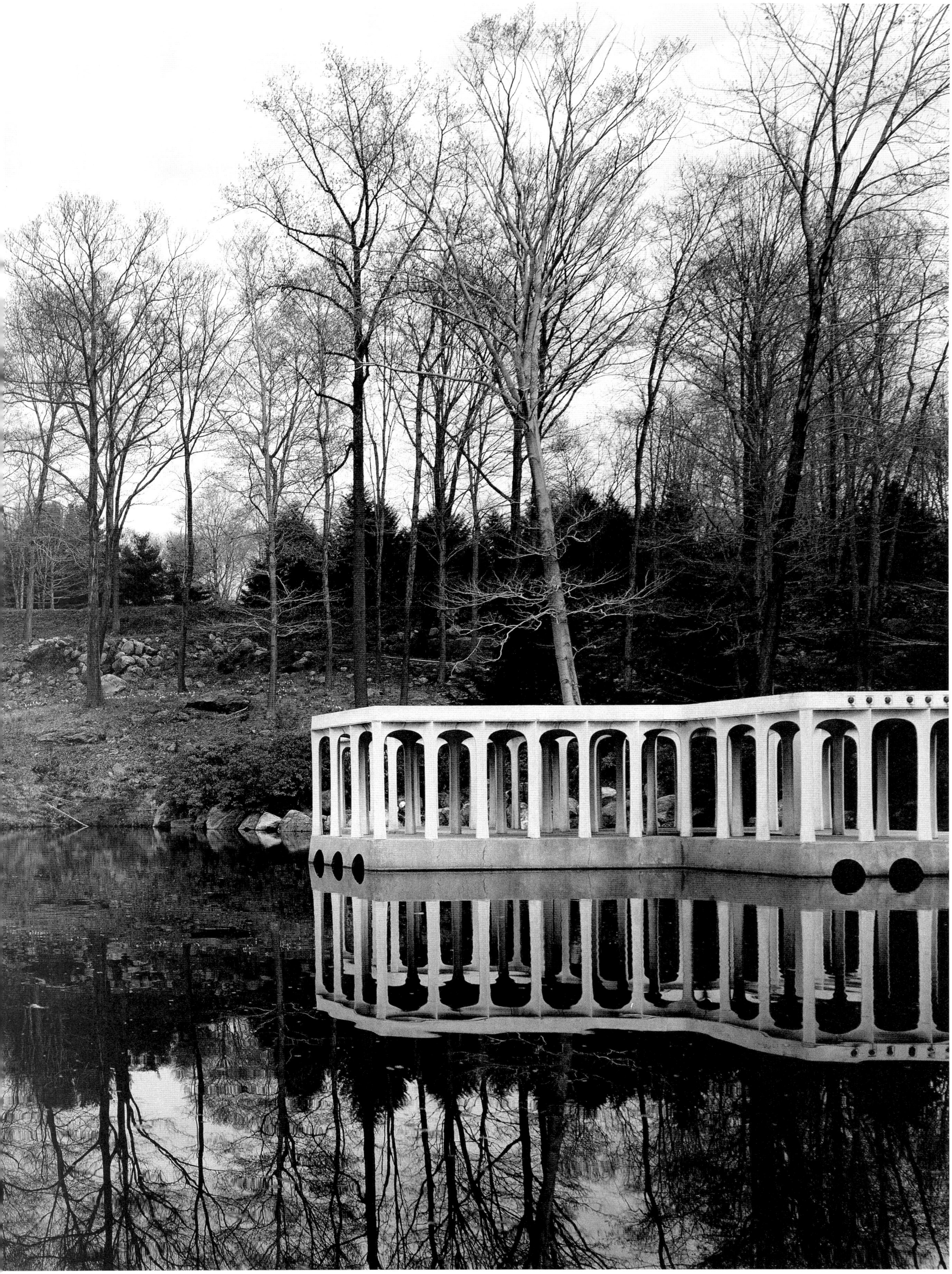

View toward Pavilion in the Pond and Monument to Lincoln Kirstein (1985) from Glass House

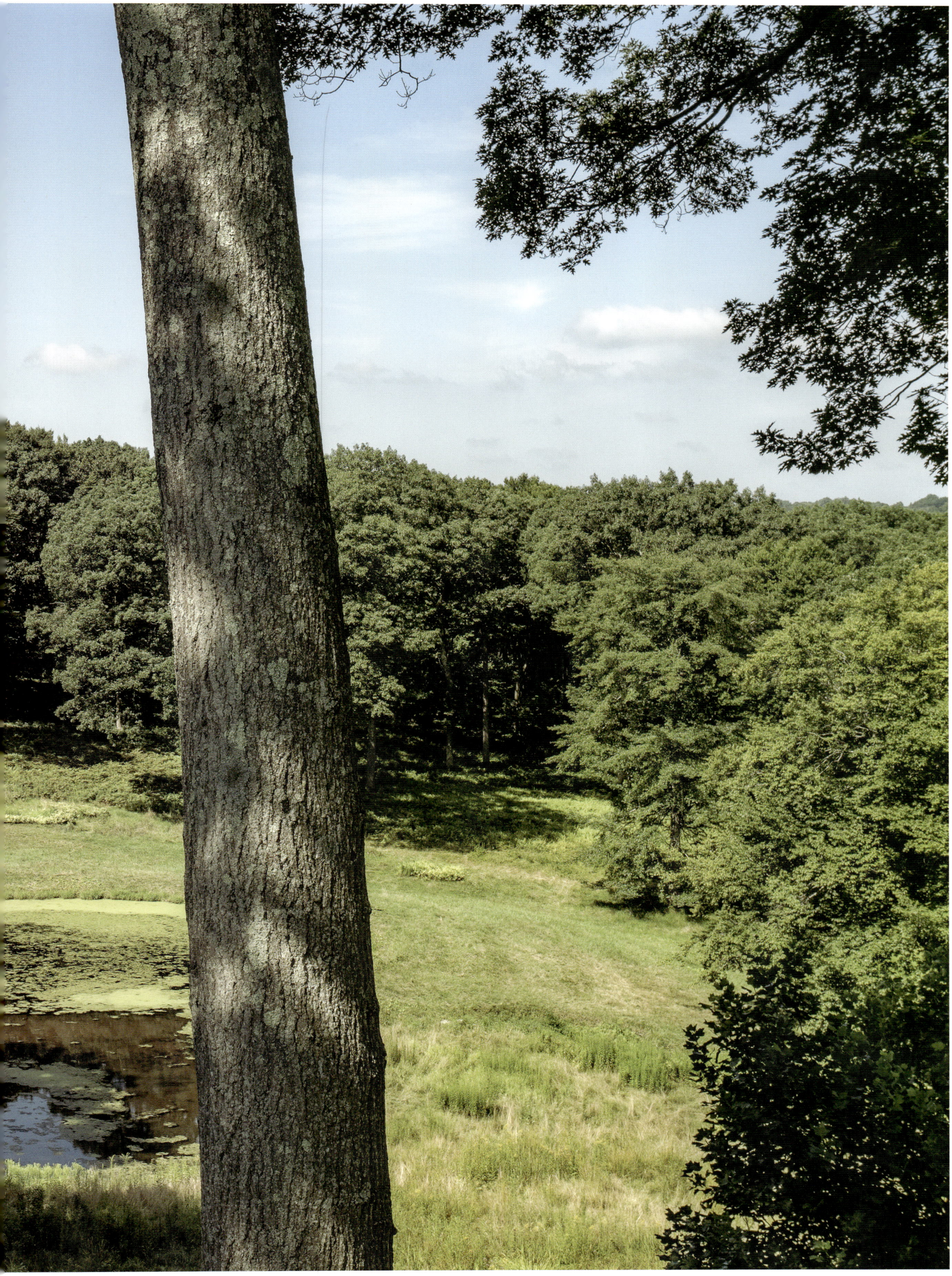

世界現代住宅全集19
フィリップ・ジョンソン
グラス・ハウス

2015年7月24日発行
文：隈研吾
撮影：二川幸夫
編集：二川由夫
アート・ディレクション：細谷巖
印刷・製本：大日本印刷株式会社
制作・発行：エーディーエー・エディタ・トーキョー
151-0051　東京都渋谷区千駄ヶ谷3-12-14
TEL.(03) 3403-1581 (代)

禁無断転載
ISBN 978-4-87140-644-4 C1352